चण्डी पाठः
Chaṇḍī Pāṭhaḥ
She Who Tears Apart Thought

Also Known As

The Durgā Saptaśatī
The Seven Hundred Verses
In Praise of She Who Removes
All Difficulties

And

The Devī Māhātmyam
The Glory of the Goddess

Study of Chapter One

Translated By
स्वामी सत्यानन्द सरस्वती
Swami Satyananda Saraswati
श्री माँ
Shree Maa

Chaṇḍī Pāṭh, **Study of Chapter One** First edition

ISBN 1-877795-58-5
Library of Congress Catalog

Chaṇḍī Pāṭh, Swami Satyananda Saraswati
1. Hindu Religion. 2. Goddess Worship. 3. Spirituality.
4. Philosophy. I. Saraswati, Swami Satyananda.

Published by
Devi Mandir Publications
5950 Highway 128
Napa, CA 94558 USA
707-966-2802
www.shreemaa.org

Introduction

What a great privilege it is to be able to share a major portion of the fruit of our tapasya, our current understanding of the *Chandi Path*. This is a marvelous opportunity for which we thank you all.

We also want to thank Parvati, who has transcribed and edited with so much love, hours of discussions from years of classes and discourses shared around the world.

We recognize that this is only the first chapter from the *Chandi Path*, and that much more is left to be completed. But this is a start, and we pray it will inspire our family as we strive to complete the project.

We pray for blessings from the Divine Mother, that all of us are filled with love, light, wisdom, peace, and discrimination, and we give you all our blessings and respect and any assistance that we can offer to make your journey more efficient.

Mrikanda Muni, Markandeya's father performed tremendous austerities to get a son from Shiva. After some time Lord Shiva appeared to him and asked him what boon he wanted. Mrikanda told Shiva that he wanted a son. Shiva said to him, "You can have a foolish son with a long life or you can have a very intelligent son, but he will die at an early age." Mrikanda Muni said, "I'll take the intelligent son." So Markandeya was born as the son of Mrikanda Muni and Mrikanda Muni was very happy.

Markandeya grew up as a lover of Shiva. His father gave him a lot of knowledge and taught him how to do tapasya. When his son reached sixteen years of age, Mrikanda became very sad because he knew that his son was destined to die. Then the Muni decided that he didn't want to live in the world without his son, and so he resolved to take his own life. Just then Narada Muni appeared and asked him why he was trying to die. Mrikanda Muni explained that he was very sad that his son was destined to die. When Markandeya overheard this, he said to his father, "It is okay, Father. This body is made up of the five elements and it is not eternal. Why are you sad when you have so much knowledge? Mrikanḍa answered, "Because I will not be able to see you any more."

Narad Muni then told Markandeya, "If you perform

austerities for Lord Shiva, He will give you blessings. Shiva brought you here and only Shiva will take you from here."

So Markandeya went off to perform tapasya. He began to worship Shiva everyday, twenty-four hours a day. He recited the Mahamrityunjaya Mantra, the mantra which gives victory over death. At the appointed time Yama, the God of Death, sent his servants to take Markandeya. But Markandeya was completely absorbed in samadhi, and they were unable.

Then the God of Death himself came. He pulled at the young boy with all his might. Markandeya grabbed on to the Shiva Lingam. The God of Death continued to pull. Then Shiva appeared and said, "You cannot take the boy. He was praying to me with pure devotion, and has completely surrendered to me."

Yama said, "But it is my duty to take him. It says in my book that his time has come. What should I do?"

Shiva said, "No, you cannot take him. He will not go with you until I say to take him."

Just then the Divine Mother appeared. She told Yama, "You cannot take him. I will give him a boon." And She told Markandeya, "You will write about me and you will share that knowledge with all of humanity so they will understand how they can be united with me. When they will know about me, they will be able to live in peace."

So Markandeya was saved and he went off to perform greater tapasya to realize the Divine Mother. After his realization he wrote the *Chandi Path*.

श्री दुर्गायै नमः

śrī durgāyai namaḥ

We bow to She who Removes All Difficulties

अथ श्रीदुर्गासप्तशती

atha śrī durgā saptaśatī

And Now,
The Seven Hundred Verses in Praise of
She Who Removes all Difficulties

प्रथमोऽध्यायः

prathamo-dhyāyaḥ

Chapter One

विनियोगः

viniyogaḥ

Application

ॐ प्रथमचरित्रस्य ब्रह्मा ऋषिः महाकाली देवता गायत्री छन्दः नन्दा शक्तिः रक्तदन्तिका बीजम् अग्निस्तत्त्वम् ऋग्वेदः स्वरूपम् श्रीमहाकालीप्रीत्यर्थे प्रथमचरित्रजपे विनियोगः ।

oṃ prathama caritrasya brahmā ṛṣiḥ mahākālī devatā gāyatrī chandaḥ nandā śaktiḥ raktadantikā bījam agnistattvam ṛgvedaḥ svarūpam śrī mahākālī prītyarthe prathama caritra jape viniyogaḥ |

Oṃ Presenting the first episode, the Creative Capacity is the Seer, the Great Remover of Darkness is the deity, Gāyatrī (24 syllables to the verse) is the meter, Nandā is the energy, Raktadantikā is the seed, Fire is the principle, Ṛg Veda is the intrinsic nature, and for the satisfaction of the Great Remover of Darkness this first episode is being applied in recitation.

ध्यानम्

dhyānam
Meditation

खड्गं चक्रगदेषुचापपरिघाञ्छूलं भुशुण्डीं शिरः
शङ्खं संदधतीं करैस्त्रिनयनां सर्वाङ्गभूषावृताम् ।
नीलाश्मद्युतिमास्यपाददशकां सेवे महाकालिकां
यामस्तौत्स्वपिते हरौ कमलजो हन्तुं मधुं कैटभम् ॥

khaḍgaṃ cakra gadeṣu cāpa
parighāñ chūlaṃ bhuśuṇḍīṃ śiraḥ
śaṅkhaṃ saṃdadhatīṃ karai
strinayanāṃ sarvāṅga bhūṣāvṛtām |
nīlāśmadyutimāsya pāda
daśakāṃ seve mahākālikāṃ
yāmastaut svapite harau kamalajo
hantuṃ madhuṃ kaiṭabham ||

Bearing in Her ten hands the sword of worship, the discus of revolving time, the club of articulation, the bow of determination, the iron bar of restraint, the pike of attention, the sling, the head of egotism, and the conch of vibrations, She has three eyes and displays ornaments on all Her limbs. Shining like a blue gem, She has ten faces. I worship that Great Remover of Darkness whom the lotus-born Creative Capacity praised in order to slay Too Much and Too Little, when the Supreme Consciousness was in sleep.

ॐ नमश्चण्डिकायै

oṃ namaścaṇḍikāyai

oṃ Oṃ

namaś We bow

caṇḍikāyai to She Who Tears Apart Thought

Oṃ We bow to She Who Tears Apart Thought.

- 1 -

ॐ ऐं मार्कण्डेय उवाच ॥

oṃ aiṃ mārkaṇḍeya uvāca ||

oṃ aiṃ Oṃ Aiṃ

mārkaṇḍeya Mārkaṇḍeya

uvāca || said:

Oṃ Aiṃ Mārkaṇḍeya said:

- 2 -

सावर्णिः सूर्यतनयो यो मनुः कथ्यतेऽष्टमः ।
निशामय तदुत्पत्तिं विस्तराद् गदतो मम ॥

sāvarṇiḥ sūryatanayo yo manuḥ kathyate-ṣṭamaḥ |
niśāmaya tadutpattiṃ vistarād gadato mama ||

sā He, with

varṇiḥ colors, tribes, and castes

sūrya Sun, Light of Wisdom

tanayo the son of

yo he

manuḥ Manifestation of Wisdom

kathyate is known as

-ṣṭamaḥ | eighth

niśāmaya this idea, story

tad his

utpattiṃ origins

vistarād described

gadato at length

mama || by me

He who belongs to all colors, tribes, and castes, the son of the Light of Wisdom, is known as the eighth Manifestation of Wisdom. I describe his origins at length. Listen.

Markandeya Muni was performing tapasya with his four disciples. One night one of the disciples asked him, "There are fourteen manvantaras, periods of time, with a Manu presiding over each one, a predominant attitude of mind. We are now in the Eighth Manvantara and the name of the Manu is Savarni. How did Savarni become the Manu of this manvantara?" That is the question we will propose to answer in the *Chandi Path*.

Savarni means he who belongs to all colors, castes, tribes, and creeds, he who belongs to everyone. There are four yugas: Sattva, Dvarpara, Treta, and Kali Yugas. One revolution of the four yugas is called a kalpa, and seventh-one kalpas is a manvantara. One manvantara is a day of Brahma and one manvantara is a night of Brahma. Two manvantaras are equal to a day and a night of Brahma. There are fourteen manvantaras in a period of time of Brahma and then they repeat. Please examine the following calculations.

The Calculations of Time and the Manus

Narayana then gives the divisions of time from the minutest, namely the Lava to the duration of Brahma's life (or a period of 36,000 days and nights, each of 8,640,000,000 human years duration) as follows:

1 Lava = the time it takes to pierce the film on a lotus leaf with a needle.

30 Lavas = 1 Truti.

30 Trutis = 1 Kalaa.

30 Kalaas = 1 Kaashthaa.

30 Kaashthaas = 1 Nimesha (blink of an eye).

8 Nimeshas = 1 Maatraa which is equal to one breath (Shvaasa).

360 Shvaasas = 1 Danda or Naadikaa.

2 Naadikaas = 1 Murhuurtta.

30 Muhuurtas = 1 day and night.

30 days and nights = 1 month.

12 months = 1 human year.

1 human year = 1 day and night of the Devas.

360 days of the Devas = 1 celestial year.

12,000 celestial years = 1 Kalpa (Four Yugas).
1,000 Kalpas = 1 day of Brahma.
1,000 Kalpas = 1 night of Brahma.
30 such days and nights of Brahma = 1 month of Brahma.
12 months of Brahma = 1 year of Brahma.
100 years of Brahma = the period of the life of Brahma.
The duration of Brahma's life = that of the outgoing breath (nishvaasa) of Kaala, (Narayana).

Prapanchasara Tantra, page 8

The duration of Satya Yuga is 1,728,000 years.

Three fourths of of this period. 1,296,000 years is the duration of Treta Yuga.

Half of the duration of Satya Yuga, 864,000, is the duration of Dvapara, and a fourth of it, 432,000 years, is the duration of Kali Yuga.

4,320,000 years is the duration of a Kalpa, one revolution of the four Yugas.

Tantraraja Tantra, page 46.

A Manvantara is 1/14th part of a day of Brahma.
71 Kalpas (71 times the four Yugas) = 1 Manvantara.
14 Manvantaras = 1,000 Kalpas = 1 day of Brahma.

Each Manvantara is presided over by one Manu, the manifestation of the predominant attitude of mind for that period.

We are now in the Eighth Manvantara. There have been eight Manus that have manifested so far:

1. Svayambhubha
2. Svarochisa
3. Uttama
4. Tamasa
5. Raivata
6. Chakshusa
7. Vaivashvata
8. Savarni

Savarni is the Manu of the present Manvantara. The *Chandi Path* tells the story of how he became the Manu of this period of time. In the second Manvantara, the period ruled by Svarochisa, Savarni was the King of Good Thoughts. Good Thoughts performed a severe tapasya, and the Divine Mother Goddess granted him an imperishable kingdom. So Good Thoughts became the predominant attitude of mind for this period of 71 Kalpas, or if you do the math: 306,720,000 years.

- 3 -

महामायानुभावेन यथा मन्वन्तराधिपः ।
स बभूव महाभागः सावर्णिस्तनयो रवेः ॥

mahāmāyā nubhāvena yathā manvantarādhipaḥ I
sa babhūva mahā bhāgaḥ sāvarṇistanayo raveḥ II

mahāmāyā the Great Measurement of Consciousness
anubhāvena by means of Her most subtle feeling, (of the attitude of an atom) grace
yathā thence
manvantar of the fourteenth part of a day of the Infinite
ādhipaḥ I master
sa he
babhūva became
mahā bhāgaḥ highly eminent
sāvarṇis He Who Belongs to All
tanayo raveḥ II the son of the Sun.

With the grace of the Supreme Goddess, the Great Measurement of Consciousness, the son of the Light, He Who Belongs to All, became the highly eminent master of the fourteenth part of a day of the Infinite. (On this subject I speak.)

- 4 -

स्वारोचिषऽन्तरे पूर्वं चैत्रवंशसमुद्भवः ।
सुरथो नाम राजाभूत्समस्ते क्षितिमण्डले ॥

svārociṣe-ntare pūrvaṃ caitravaṃśa samudbhavaḥ I
suratho nāma rājābhūt samaste kṣiti maṇḍale II

svārociṣe He who makes Himself Radiant
-ntare in the period ruled by
pūrvaṃ In times of old
caitra those Who Dwell in Consciousness
vaṃśa of the lineage
samudbhavaḥ I born

suratho Conveyor of Good Thoughts
nāma named
rājābhūt a King with authority over the earth
samaste all
kṣiti earth
maṇḍale || the regions
In times of old, in the period ruled by He who makes Himself Radiant, there was a King named the Conveyor of Good Thoughts, born of the lineage of Those Who Dwell in Consciousness, and he had authority over all the regions of the earth.

Markandeya, the guru, began to tell this story to his disciples. "In olden days the second manvantara was presided over by Svarochisa, He or She who continually fills his or her own self with delight, or who is delighted just being herself or himself, or who makes herself or himself radiant.

At that time there was a king named Suratha, the Conveyance of Excellence, or Good Thoughts. Good Thoughts had dominion over the entire earth. There was never a bad thought allowed in his kingdom.

- 5 -

तस्य पालयतः सम्यक् प्रजाः पुत्रानिवौरसान् ।
बभूवुः शत्रवो भूपाः कोलाविध्वंसिनस्तदा ॥

tasya pālayataḥ samyak prajāḥ putrā nivaurasān |
babhūvuḥ śatravo bhūpāḥ kolā vidhvaṃsi nastadā ||

tasya his
pālayataḥ He protected
samyak complete control, dharma, in the Way of Truth
prajāḥ subjects
putrā children
nivaurasān | as they were dependents, as a father
babhūvuḥ became
śatravo enemies
bhūpāḥ kings who
kolā highest excellence of worship

vidhvaṃsi the appendages of knowledge
nastadā || destroy
He protected his subjects in the Way of Truth as a father to his children. At that time the kings who were the Destroyers of Worship became his enemies.

Then one time the kings who were the destroyers of worship became his enemies and attacked. These kings are the ripus or limitations of consciousness for individuals: kama - desire, krodh - anger, labh - greed, moha - ignorance born of attachments, modha - foolishness, matsarya - envy or jealousy. These Destroyers of Worship said, "It is not necessary to meditate today. You are too busy. You don't have enough time." The Destroyers of Worship attacked the appendages of knowledge: vyakaran - grammar; uccharan - pronunciation; itihas/sahitya - history/literature; darshan shashtra - philosophy; jyotish - astrology; paddhoti - systems of worship.

- 6 -

तस्य तैरभवद् युद्धमतिप्रबलदण्डिनः ।
न्यूनैरपि स तैर्युद्धे कोलाविध्वंसिभिर्जितः ॥

tasya tairabhavad yuddham ati prabala daṇḍinaḥ |
nyūnairapi sa tairyuddhe kolāvidhvaṃsibhirjitaḥ ||

tasya his
tair them
abhavad engaged
yuddham battle
ati extremely
prabala strong
daṇḍinaḥ | punish, attacked
nyūnairapi nevertheless
sa he
tair them
yuddhe battle
kolāvidhvaṃsi Destroyers of Worship
bhirjitaḥ || was defeated

Good Thoughts moved against the Destroyers of Worship to engage in battle, and even though they were fewer in numbers, nevertheless Good Thoughts was defeated.

Even though he had greater numbers in his forces, he was defeated. There were so many good thoughts to contemplate, while the kings who were his enemies were only six. Nevertheless, they defeated Good Thoughts.

- 7 -

ततः स्वपुरमायातो निजदेशाधिपोऽभवत् ।

आक्रान्तः स महाभागस्तैस्तदा प्रबलारिभिः ॥

tataḥ svapura māyāto nija deśā dhipo-bhavat |

ākrāntaḥ sa mahā bhāgas taistadā prabalāribhiḥ ||

tataḥ then

svapura to his own city

māyāto he returned

nija his own

deśa land

ādhipo-bhavat | continued to rule

ākrāntaḥ powerful enemies

sa he

mahā bhāgas illustrious one

taistadā but there, too,

prabal powerful

āribhiḥ || again attacked.

Then he returned to his own city, renouncing his authority over the earth, and continued to rule in his own land. But there, too, the powerful enemies pursued that illustrious one and again attacked.

Then he returned to his own kingdom, and locked the nine gates by which to enter: two eyes, two ears, two nostrils, mouth, reproductive organ, and anus.

- 8 -

अमात्यैर्बलिभिर्दुष्टैर्दुर्बलस्य दुरात्मभिः ।
कोशो बलं चापहृतं तत्रापि स्वपुरे ततः ॥

amātyair balibhir duṣṭair durbalasya durātmabhiḥ |
kośo balaṃ cāpahṛtaṃ tatrāpi svapure tataḥ ||

amātyair the King's or his severely depleted
balibhir strength
duṣṭair enemies
dur were evil
balasya and mighty
durātmabhiḥ | evil souls, unscrupulous ministers
kośo the treasury
balaṃ strength
cāpa took over
hṛtaṃ joy
tatrāpi and protection
svapure in his city
tataḥ || there

The King's strength was severely depleted, his enemies were mighty, and his unscrupulous ministers took over the army and the treasury.

The King's unscrupulous ministers are his conscience.

- 9 -

ततो मृगयाव्याजेन हृतस्वाम्यः स भूपतिः ।
एकाकी हयमारुह्य जगाम गहनं वनम् ॥

tato mṛgayāvyājena hṛtasvāmyaḥ sa bhūpatiḥ |
ekākī hayamāruhya jagāma gahanaṃ vanam ||

tato his
mṛgayāvyājena left with the speed of a deer
hṛtasvāmyaḥ joy of the family
sa he
bhūpatiḥ | kingship, king of earth, sovereignty
ekākī riding alone

haya horse
māruhya upon
jagāma he fled
gahanaṃ hunt
vanam || into the dense forest
Good Thought's sovereignty was lost, and therefore riding alone upon his horse, he fled into the dense forest on the pretext of hunting.

\- 10 -

स तत्राश्रममद्राक्षीद् द्विजवर्यस्य मेधसः ।
प्रशान्तश्वापदाकीर्णं मुनिशिष्योपशोभितम् ॥

sa tatrāśramamadrākṣīd dvija varyasya medhasaḥ |
praśāntaśvā padākīrṇaṃ muni śiṣyo paśobhitam ||

sa he
tatra there
āśramam the hermitage, place of refuge
adrākṣīd he came upon
dvija a great wise master, twice born
varyasya dangerous animals
medhasaḥ | the Intellect of Love
praśāntaśvā he saw
padākīrṇaṃ magnificence, radiance
muni Great Wise One
śiṣyo disciples
paśobhitam || enhancing, illuminating
There he came upon the hermitage of a great wise master, the Intellect of Love, where he saw so many dangerous animals living together in the greatest of peace. Many disciples to the Great Wise One were enhancing the magnificence of the forest.

\- 11 -

तस्थौ कंचित्स कालं च मुनिना तेन सत्कृतः ।
इतश्चेतश्च विचरंस्तस्मिन्मुनिवराश्रमे ॥

tasthau kaṃcitsa kālaṃ ca muninā tena satkṛtaḥ |
itaśce taśca vicaraṃs tasmin muni varāśrame ||

tasthau there
kaṃcitsa some
kālaṃ time
ca and
muninā the Great Wise One
tena him
satkṛtaḥ | welcome, with truthful activity, respect
itaśce taśca here and there
vicaraṃs wandered
tasmin there
muni The Great Wise One
var respected
āśrame || about the hermitage
The Great Wise One made him welcome there with respect, and the King wandered about the hermitage for some time.

- 12 -

सोऽचिन्तयत्तदा तत्र ममत्वाकृष्टचेतनः ।
मत्पूर्वैः पालितं पूर्वं मया हीनं पुरं हि तत् ॥

so-cintayat tadā tatra mamatvā kṛṣṭa cetanaḥ |
matpūrvaiḥ pālitaṃ pūrvaṃ
mayā hīnaṃ puraṃ hi tat ||

so- he
cintayat thoughts
tadā then
tatra there
mamatvā attachment
kṛṣṭa desired, egotistical, doing with attachment
cetanaḥ | consciousness, contemplations
mat my
pūrvaiḥ of ancestors
pālitaṃ protected
pūrvaṃ in times of old
mayā from me

hīnaṃ gone
puraṃ city
hi tat || that
Then his contemplations were overcome with egotism and attachment, and he thought, "The city that my ancestors protected in former times has now gone from me.

- 13 -

मद्भृत्यैस्तैरसद्वृत्तैर्धर्मतः पाल्यते न वा ।
न जाने स प्रधानो मे शूरहस्ती सदामदः ॥

madbhṛtyais tairasad vṛttair
dharmataḥ pālyate na vā |
na jāne sa pradhāno me śūrahastī sadāmadaḥ ||

mad my
bhṛtyaistair the kingdom
asad unprincipled
vṛttair employees, performers of action
dharmataḥ righteously, in the way of truth, in the highest ideal of perfection
pālyate preserving
na not
vā | or
na jāne I don't know
sa he
pradhāno foremost
me my
śūrahastī elephant
sadā continually
madaḥ || delighted
Are my unprincipled employees protecting and righteously preserving the kingdom in my absence? And my foremost elephant, heroic and continually delighted,

- 14 -

मम वैरिवशं यातः कान् भोगानुपलप्स्यते ।
ये ममानुगता नित्यं प्रसादधनभोजनैः ॥

mama vairivaśaṃ yātaḥ kān bhogānupalapsyate |
ye mamānugatā nityaṃ prasāda dhana bhojanaiḥ ||

mama my
vairivaśaṃ during my reign
yātaḥ as he had
kān will
bhog the pleasures
ānupalapsyate | enjoyed
ye those
mama me
anugatā followed
nityaṃ eternal
prasāda offering
dhana wealth
bhojanaiḥ || food

will not experience the pleasures he enjoyed during my time. Those who followed me with the eternal way of offering wealth and food,

- 15 -

अनुवृत्तिं ध्रुवं तेऽद्य कुर्वन्त्यन्यमहीभृताम् ।
असम्यग्व्ययशीलैस्तैः कुर्वद्भिः सततं व्ययम् ॥

anuvṛttiṃ dhruvaṃ te-dya
kurvantyan yamahībhṛtām |
asamyagvyayaśīlaistaiḥ
kurvadbhiḥ satataṃ vyayam ||

anuvṛttiṃ subtle changes
dhruvaṃ definitely
te-dya them, the other kings
kurvantyan now serving
yama hībhṛtām | without restraint

asamyagvyaya extravagance
śīlaistaiḥ steadfast
kurvadbhiḥ are spending
satatam continual
vyayam || may be
definitely may now be serving other kings, who are spending without restraint in continual extravagance."

- 16 -

संचितः सोऽतिदुःखेन क्षयं कोशो गमिष्यति ।
एतच्चान्यच्च सततं चिन्तयामास पार्थिवः ॥

saṃcitaḥ so-tiduḥkhena kṣayaṃ kośo gamiṣyati |
etaccānyacca satataṃ cintayāmāsa pārthivaḥ ||

saṃcitaḥ deeper contemplation
so he
-tiduḥkhena in great pain
kṣayaṃ his attachments
kośo wealth
gamiṣyati | absorbed
etac his present situation
ca and
anyac other
ca and
satataṃ always
cintayāmāsa thoughts
pārthivaḥ || the King
And as the King went into deeper contemplation of the loss of his wealth and his present situation, his mind became absorbed in pain and his thoughts controlled by worldly attachments.

- 17 -

तत्र विप्राश्रमाभ्याशे वैश्यमेकं ददर्श सः ।
स पृष्टस्तेन कस्त्वं भो हेतुश्चागमनेऽत्र कः ॥

tatra viprāśram ābhyāśe vaiśyamekaṃ dadarśa saḥ |
sa pṛṣṭastena kastvaṃ bho hetuścāgamane-tra kaḥ ||

tatra there
vipra the great teacher, twice-born
āśramābhyāśe in the hermitage (locative)
vaiśyam businessman
ekaṃ a (one)
dadarśa saw
saḥ | he
sa he
pṛṣṭastena greeting
kastvaṃ who are you
bho after
hetuś motivation, purpose
ca and
āgamane-tra your coming here
kaḥ || what

There in the hermitage of the great teacher he saw a businessman, and after greeting him, asked, "Who are you, and what is the reason for your coming here?

- 18 -

सशोक इव कस्मात्त्वं दुर्मना इव लक्ष्यसे ।
इत्याकर्ण्य वचस्तस्य भूपतेः प्रणयोदितम् ॥

saśoka iva kasmāttvaṃ durmanā iva lakṣyase |
ityākarṇya vacastasya bhūpateḥ praṇayoditam ||

sa he
śoka great sorrow, grief
iva as though
kasmāttvaṃ you appear
dur far
manā mind
iva as though
lakṣyase | from goal
iti thus
yākarṇya pleasant spirit
vacastasya asked to him

bhūpateḥ the King
praṇayoditam || with respect
Why do you appear to be in a great sorrow as though your mind were far from its goal?" asked the King in a pleasant voice and friendly spirit.

- 19 -

प्रत्युवाच स तं वैश्यः प्रश्रयावनतो नृपम् ॥

pratyuvāca sa taṃ vaiśyaḥ praśrayāvanato nṛpam ||
praty fully
uvāca replied
sa he
taṃ to him
vaiśyaḥ businessman
praśrayāvanato modesty and humble respect
nṛpam || to the King
And with words full of modesty and humble respect, the businessman replied to the King.

- 20 -

वैश्य उवाच ॥

vaiśya uvāca ||
vaiśya the Businessman
uvāca || said:
The Businessman said:

- 21 -

समाधिर्नाम वैश्योऽहमुत्पन्नो धनिनां कुले ॥

samādhirnāma vaiśyo-hamutpanno dhaninām kule ||
samādhir Pure Intuitive Perception, all - measurement - mind
nāma name
vaiśyo businessman
-ham I am
utpanno born
dhaninām of the wealth
kule || in the lineage of those who worship Infinite Energy

Pure Intuitive Perception is my name, and I'm a businessman born in the lineage of those who worship Infinite Energy.

There are three types of samadhi. Bhava samadhi is an attitude, an intensity of awareness, a contemplation about the recipient of your love. In Bhava three things exist: subject aham, object twam, and their relationship, for example, "I am your devotee" or "I love you." There are two types of this samadhi described in Samskrit literature. The first is salokya. Loka means world. In our usage it means a paradigm of reality. Sa means with or in the same world: in immediate proximity to each other, in the same paradigm of reality and togetherness. It can be physical or metaphysical, but there is togetherness. You are in the same plane of reality together with your beloved.

The second kind of Bhava Samadhi is called samipya. Just as you are doing, so I am also doing. We are performing the same karma. I see you, the Goddess, sitting there performing pranayama, breathing love into the entire universe, and I am sitting here performing the same pranayama, making japa of the same mantra, breathing the same love into the universe. You and I are one in the performance of the same activity. These are the two types of Bhava Samadhi.

The second kind of samadhi is called Savikalpa Samadhi, which means with a form that can be thought. Sa means with and vikalpa is with an idea. Savikalpa is with an idea that I am and you are separate and distinct entities. Savikalpa has two types of samadhi. Sarupa means with form. I have an idea that your form and my form are alike. I look at you and it is like looking in a mirror. You and I have the same form. I have an idea of aham-twam, separation between you and I, but the relationship is understood. In bhava samadhi there are three things: subject, object, and the relationship between them. In savikalpa there are only two things, subject and object. The relationship is not intellectual. Intuitively, I see sarupa, I see the form. I am looking in the mirror. I see you, my deity, my perfect reflection.

Sadristi means with perception. Just as I am perceiving you, so you are perceiving me. Which one is the reality, and which one is the reflection? Who can say? There is no one else. There is no other relationship by which to define.

The third type of samadhi is called Nirvikalpa Samadhi. Nir means water: with the idea of water. Water is always in equilibrium, it is always balanced. It is always in harmony. Nir also means without - without an idea. There is only one form of

Nirvikalpa Samadhi called sayuja. Yuja means union. Sa means with: the perfection of union. Nirvikalpa either means with the idea of the perfect balance or it means without any idea. That is the Vedic sayings, "Aham Brahmasmi" or "tat twam asi." It is all aham or it is all twam. But there is no other option. In Nirvikalpa Samadhi there is one aspect called sayuga. With union. There is no duality, there is no separation at all. We are one.

Bhava, savikalpa, nirvikalpa, salokya, samipya, sarupa, sadristi, sayuja. These are the different forms of prakasha. Salokya is in the same paradigm of reality. Samipya is in the same activity. Sarupa is having the same appearance. Sadristi is having the same perception. Sayuja means that we are the same. These are the five kinds of prakasha, illumination, experienced in meditation.

The businessman was born in the lineage of those who worship Infinite Energy, those who are practicianers of Kolachara, the behavior of excellence.

- 22 -

पुत्रदारैर्निरस्तश्च धनलोभादसाधुभिः ।
विहीनश्च धनैर्दारैः पुत्रैरादाय मे धनम् ॥

putradārair nirastaśca dhana lobhāda sādhubhiḥ |
vihīnaśca dhanairdāraiḥ putrairādāya me dhanam ||

putra children
dārair wife
nirastaś put me out
ca and
dhana for wealth
lobhāda greed
sādhubhiḥ | sadhu, an ascetic Seeker of Truth.
vihīnaś deprived
ca and
dhanair wealth
dāraiḥ my wife
putrair children
ādāya estate, possessions
me my
dhanam || wealth

My wife and children have cast me out because of their greed for wealth, and have caused me to become an ascetic Seeker of Truth. I have been deprived of wealth, and my wife and sons have seized my estate,

The sons of Samadhi are all of the thoughts and reflections that appear on the stage of consciousness. When Samadhi is completely in samadhi, he perceives infinitely. If you put an object in front of that perception, he perceives finitely. He has lost his business. So now Samadhi and Good Thoughts have taken refuge in the ashram of the Intellect of Love. Look at all the Samadhis that are in the forest in the Intellect of Love. How many of us are thinking about what our children and families are doing and about all of our attachments in the outside world. Both of them sat down on the bank of the river and shared their stories.

- 23 -

वनमभ्यागतो दुःखी निरस्तश्चाप्तबन्धुभिः ।
सोऽहं न वेद्मि पुत्राणां कुशलाकुशलात्मिकाम् ॥

vanamabhyāgato duḥkhī nirastaścāpta bandhubhiḥ |
so-haṃ na vedmi putrāṇāṃ kuśalākuśalāt mikām ||

vanamabhya into the forest
āgato I have come
duḥkhī sorrow
nirastaścāpta having been cast out
bandhubhiḥ | bound
so-haṃ I and my nature
na don't
vedmi know
putrāṇāṃ children
kuśal happiness
ākuśala unhappiness
ātmikām || souls are manifesting

and having been cast out by my trusted kinsmen and bound by sorrow, I have come into the forest. But now I don't know if happiness or unhappiness is with my children.

- 24 -

प्रवृत्तिं स्वजनानां च दाराणां चात्र संस्थितः ।
किं नु तेषां गृहे क्षेममक्षेमं किं नु साम्प्रतम् ॥

pravṛttiṃ svajanānāṃ ca dārāṇāṃ cātra saṃsthitaḥ |
kiṃ nu teṣāṃ gṛhe kṣema
makṣemaṃ kiṃ nu sāmpratam ||

pravṛttiṃ activities
svajanānāṃ of my family
ca and
dārāṇāṃ I am unaware
cātra here
saṃsthitaḥ | staying, residing
kiṃ do
nu teṣāṃ they
gṛhe in their home
kṣemam tranquility
akṣemaṃ disruption
kiṃ do
nu sāmpratam || experience

Staying here I am unaware of the activities of my family. Do they experience tranquility at present or does discomfort reign?

- 25 -

कथं ते किं नु सद्वृत्ता दुर्वृत्ताः किं नु मे सुताः ॥

kathaṃ te kiṃ nu sad vṛttā
durvṛttāḥ kiṃ nu me sutāḥ ||

kathaṃ knowledge, story, speak
te they
kiṃ do
nu sad vṛttā truthful behavior
durvṛttāḥ evil behavior
kiṃ do
nu me my
sutāḥ || sons

Are my sons observing good conduct, or are they behaving with evil and wickedness?

Then they said to each other. "Isn't it strange this ashram is such a beautiful place of refuge. The fruits are so sweet, the food is delicious. There is nothing lacking here. Why are our minds thinking about all the stuff we left behind? Why can't we make our minds sit still in the present reality? Why are we clinging to attachments of the past? The king is thinking about his elephant and about his kingdom, his ministers, and all his wealth. Samadhi is thinking about his children. He is wondering if they are happy now that they have stolen all his wealth and thrown him out.

- 26 -

राजोवाच ॥

rājovāca ||

rāja The King
uvāca || said:
The King said:

- 27 -

यैर्निरस्तो भवांल्लुब्धैः पुत्रदारादिभिर्धनैः ॥

yairnirasto bhavāṃllubdhaiḥ
putradārādibhir dhanaiḥ ||

yair you
nirasto have been cast out
bhavāṃllubdhaiḥ because of their avarice and greed
putra children
dārādibhir by your wife
dhanaiḥ || for wealth
You have been cast out by your wife and children because of their avarice and greed;

- 28 -

तेषु किं भवतः स्नेहमनुबध्नाति मानसम् ॥

teṣu kiṃ bhavataḥ sneham anubadhnāti mānasam ||

teṣu for them
kiṃ why
bhavataḥ are

sneham in love
anubadhnāti so bound
mānasam || thoughts
Why are your thoughts so bound in love for them?

- 29 -

वैश्य उवाच ॥

vaiśya uvāca ||

vaiśya the Businessman
uvāca || said:
The Businessman said:

- 30 -

एवमेतद्यथा प्राह भवानस्मद्गतं वचः ॥

evametadyathā prāha bhavānasmadgataṃ vacaḥ ||

evam this
etad same
yathā just as
prāha you were declaring
bhavān you
asmad thus
gataṃ vacaḥ || went my words, vibrations
Just as you were speaking to me I was having this same thought.

- 31 -

किं करोमि न बध्नाति मम निष्ठुरतां मनः ।
यैः संत्यज्य पितृस्नेहं धनलुब्धैर्निराकृतः ॥

kiṃ karomi na badhnāti mama niṣṭhuratāṃ manaḥ |
yaiḥ saṃtyajya pitṛsnehaṃ dhana lubdhair nirākṛtaḥ ||

kiṃ what
karomi can I do
na not
badhnāti does entertain, become bound by
mama my
niṣṭhuratāṃ severity
manaḥ | mind
yaiḥ they

saṃ completely
tyajya have sacrificed
pitṛ father's
snehaṃ love
dhana wealth
lubdhair because of greed for
nirākṛtaḥ || have not performed

- 32 -

पतिस्वजनहार्दं च हार्दि तेष्वेव मे मनः ।
किमेतन्नाभिजानामि जानन्नपि महामते ॥

patisvajanahārdaṃ ca hārdi teṣveva me manaḥ |
ki me tannābhi jānāmi jānannapi mahā mate ||

pati master
svajana kinsman, your own person
hārdaṃ love
ca and
hārdi affection
teṣveva they
me my
manaḥ | mind
ki what
me is to me
tan all this
nābhi jānāmi I fail to understand
jānannapi though knowing
mahā mate || oh Great Learned One

31-32. But what can I do? My mind does not entertain severity. They have sacrificed a father's love, and affection for a master and kinsman, in their greed for wealth, yet my mind joins them all in affection. Though knowing all this, Oh Great Learned One, I fail to understand how

- 33 -

यत्प्रेमप्रवणं चित्तं विगुणेष्वपि बन्धुषु ।
तेषां कृते मे निःश्वासो दौर्मनस्यं च जायते ॥

yat prema pravaṇaṃ cittaṃ viguṇeṣvapi bandhuṣu I
teṣāṃ kṛte me niḥśvāso daurmanasyaṃ ca jāyate II

yat how
prema to love
pravaṇaṃ are disposed
cittaṃ contemplations
viguṇeṣva characterless
api even
bandhuṣu I relations
teṣāṃ because of their
kṛte actions
me my
niḥśvāso heave a sigh
daurmanasyaṃ dejection, despair
ca and
jāyate II are born

my contemplations are disposed to love even characterless relations. Because of their actions, I heave a sigh and feel dejection and despair.

- 34 -

करोमि किं यन्न मनस्तेष्वप्रीतिषु निष्ठुरम् ॥

karomi kiṃ yanna manasteṣ vaprītiṣu niṣṭhuram II

karomi can I do
kiṃ what
yanna even for those
manasteṣ mind
vaprītiṣu who are devoid of love
niṣṭhuram II does not become hard

But what can I do? My mind does not become hard, even for those who are devoid of love for me.

- 35 -

मार्कण्डेय उवाच ॥

mārkaṇḍeya uvāca ||

mārkaṇḍeya Mārkaṇḍeya
uvāca || said:
Mārkaṇḍeya said:

- 36 -

ततस्तौ सहितौ विप्र तं मुनिं समुपस्थितौ ॥

tatastau sahitau vipra taṃ muniṃ samupasthitau ||

tatastau then the two
sahitau together
vipra twice born one
taṃ him
muniṃ the Great Wise Master
samupasthitau || in the presence

- 37 -

समाधिर्नाम वैश्योऽसौ स च पार्थिवसत्तमः ।
कृत्वा तु तौ यथान्यायं यथार्हं तेन संविदम् ॥

samādhirnāma vaiśyo-sau sa ca pārthiva sattamaḥ |
kṛtvā tu tau yathānyāyaṃ
yathārhaṃ tena saṃvidam ||

samādhir Pure Intuitive Perception
nāma was the name
vaiśyo-sau of the businessman
sa he
ca and
pārthiva monarch (Good Thoughts, the king)
sattamaḥ | very noble
kṛtvā observing
tu tau they
yathānyāyaṃ the proper customs
yathārhaṃ and congenialities
tena for
saṃvidam || learning

- 38 -

उपविष्टौ कथाः काश्चिच्चक्रतुर्वैश्यपार्थिवौ ॥

upaviṣṭau kathāḥ kāścic cakraturvaiśya pārthivau ||

upaviṣṭau they sat down
kathāḥ engaged in conversation
kāścic various
cakratur circular sacrificial area
vaiśya the businessman
pārthivau || the king

36-38. Then together the two, Pure Intuitive Perception, (the businessman), and the very noble monarch, (Good Thoughts, the king), arrived in the circular sacrificial area in the presence of the Great Wise Master. Observing the proper customs and congenialities for learning, they sat down and engaged in conversation.

- 39 -

राजोवाच ॥

rājovāca ||

rāja the King
uvāca || said:

The King said:

- 40 -

भगवंस्त्वामहं प्रष्टुमिच्छाम्येकं वदस्व तत् ॥

bhagavaṃstvāmahaṃ praṣṭum
icchām yekaṃ vadasva tat ||

bhagavaṃs the Infinite Self
tvām you
ahaṃ I
praṣṭum to ask
icchām wish
yekaṃ only one
vadasva please speak
tat || on that

You who have united with the Infinite Self, I wish to ask only one question of you, and please be pleased to speak on that.

- 41 -

दुःखाय यन्मे मनसः स्वचित्तायत्ततां विना ।
ममत्वं गतराज्यस्य राज्याङ्गेष्वखिलेष्वपि ॥

duḥkhāya yanme manasaḥ svacit tāyat tatāṃ vinā |
mamatvaṃ gatarājyasya rājyāṅgeṣva khileṣvapi ||

duḥkhāya give pain
yanme my
manasaḥ reflections, thoughts
svacit to my mind
tāyat control
tatāṃ that
vinā | without
mamatvaṃ attachment
gata that has gone
rājyasya to the kingdom
rājyāṅgeṣvakhileṣvapi || to every aspect of the status

My reflections are without control and give much pain to my mind. I have great attachment to the kingdom and to every aspect of the status that has gone from me.

- 42 -

जानतोऽपि यथाज्ञस्य किमेतन्मुनिसत्तम ।
अयं च निकृतः पुत्रैर्दारैर्भृत्यैस्तथोज्झितः ॥

jānato-pi yathā jñasya kimetan muni sattama |
ayaṃ ca nikṛtaḥ putrair dārair bhṛtyaistathoj jhitaḥ ||

jānato-pi even with this knowledge
yathājñasya in the manner of one who is ignorant
kimetan why is that
muni oh Great Learned One
sattama | humble man, noble, truthful man
ayaṃ this
ca and
nikṛtaḥ cheated, deceived
putrair by children

dārair by his wife
bhṛtyais by his employees, servants
tathojjhitaḥ || and cast out
But even with this knowledge, in the manner of one who is ignorant, I still feel pain. Why is that, Oh Great Learned One? And here this humble man, cheated and deceived by his wife and children and employees, and cast out;

- 43 -

स्वजनेन च संत्यक्तस्तेषु हार्दी तथाप्यति ।
एवमेष तथाहं च द्वावप्यत्यन्तदुःखितौ ॥

svajanena ca saṃtyaktas teṣu hārdī tathāpyati |
evameṣa tathāhaṃ ca dvāvap yatyanta duḥkhitau ||

svajanena by his own relations
ca and
saṃtyaktas deserted
teṣu for them
hārdī affection
tathāpyati | even
evameṣa thus
tathāhaṃ we
ca and
dvāvap both
yatyanta greatest
duḥkhitau || are feeling pain
even deserted by his own relations, he still maintains the greatest affection for them. Thus both of us are feeling pain.

- 44 -

दृष्टदोषेऽपि विषये ममत्वाकृष्टमानसौ ।
तत्किमेतन्महाभाग यन्मोहो ज्ञानिनोरपि ॥

dṛṣṭa doṣe-pi viṣaye mamatvā kṛṣṭa mānasau |
tat kimetan mahā bhāga yanmoho jñāni norapi ||

dṛṣṭa we see
doṣe the defects

-pi even
viṣaye in our contemplations
mamatvā attachment
kṛṣṭa egotism
mānasau | our minds
tat is it
kim what
etan that
mahā bhāga oh Exalted One
yan this
moho ignorance
jñāninor in the presence of our wisdom and understanding?
api || even

Even though we see the defects in our contemplations, nevertheless our minds are drawn into attachment and egotism. What is it, Oh Exalted One, that causes this ignorance, even in the presence of our wisdom and understanding?

- 45 -

ममास्य च भवत्येषा विवेकान्धस्य मूढता ॥

mamāsya ca bhavat yeṣā vivekāndhasya mūḍhatā ||

mamāsya He and I, we
ca and
bhavat become
yeṣā are as or like
vivek discrimination
āndhasya blind, without capacity
mūḍhatā || fools

He and I are as fools without the capacity of discrimination.

We all know fully well how to attain the highest realization, how to achieve the greatest wisdom: Give up all of our Attachments! Still we are like fools without the capacity of discrimination, looking for any alternative so that we can keep some of our attachments, even while we pursue liberation from all attachments.

- 46 -

ऋषिरुवाच ॥

ṛṣi ruvāca ||

ṛṣir the Ṛṣi

uvāca || said:

The Ṛṣi said:

- 47 -

ज्ञानमस्ति समस्तस्य जन्तोर्विषयगोचरे ॥

jñānamasti samastasya jantorviṣaya gocare ||

jñānam knowledge

asti is

samastasya of all

jantor that lives

viṣaya objects perceived by the senses

gocare || has

Oh Great Light of Luminous Splendor, all that lives has knowledge of objects perceived by the senses.

- 48 -

विषयश्च महाभाग याति चैवं पृथक् पृथक् ।

दिवान्धाः प्राणिनः केचिद्रात्रावन्धास्तथापरे ॥

viṣayaśca mahābhāga yāti caivaṃ pṛthak pṛthak |

divāndhāḥ prāṇinaḥ kecid rātrāvandhās tathāpare ||

viṣayaś objects of the senses

ca and

mahābhāga oh Great Light of Luminous Splendor,

yāti are perceived

caivaṃ and

pṛthak differently

pṛthak | differently

div in the day

āndhāḥ unable to see

prāṇinaḥ beings

kecid some

rātra in the night
āvandhās unable to see
tathāpare || while others
But the objects of the senses are perceived differently by all beings. Some beings are unable to see in the day, while others are unable to see in the night.

- 49 -

केचिद्दिवा तथा रात्रौ प्राणिनस्तुल्यदृष्टयः ।
ज्ञानिनो मनुजाः सत्यं किं तु ते न हि केवलम् ॥

keciddivā tathā rātrau prāṇinastulyadṛṣṭayaḥ |
jñānino manujāḥ satyaṃ kiṃ tu te na hi kevalam ||

kecid still others
divā in the day
tathā and
rātrau in the night
prāṇinas living beings
tulya equally well
dṛṣṭayaḥ | can see
jñānino a capacity of understanding
manujāḥ humans
satyaṃ it is true
kiṃ but
tu te that
na hi not
kevalam || only
Still others have the capacity to see equally well in the day and in the night. It is true that humans have a capacity of understanding, but not only humans.

- 50 -

यतो हि ज्ञानिनः सर्वे पशुपक्षिमृगादयः ।
ज्ञानं च तन्मनुष्याणां यत्तेषां मृगपक्षिणाम् ॥

yato hi jñāninaḥ sarve paśu pakṣi mṛgādayaḥ |
jñānaṃ ca tanmanuṣyāṇāṃ
yatteṣāṃ mṛgapakṣiṇām ||

yato hi this is common
jñāninaḥ knowledge
sarve to all
paśu animals
pakṣi birds of the air
mṛgādayaḥ | beasts of the forest
jñānaṃ knowledge
ca and
tan this
manuṣyāṇāṃ human beings
yatteṣāṃ is common
mṛga beasts
pakṣiṇāṃ || birds

This knowledge is common to all animals, whether beasts of the forest or birds of the air; all living beings possess this understanding just as human beings.

- 51 -

मनुष्याणां च यत्तेषां तुल्यमन्यत्तथोभयोः ।
ज्ञानेऽपि सति पश्यैतान् पतङ्गाञ्छावचञ्चुषु ॥

manuṣyāṇāṃ ca yatteṣāṃ tulyamanyat tathobhayoḥ |
jñāne-pi sati paśyaitān pataṅgāñchā vacañcuṣu ||

manuṣyāṇāṃ in humans
ca and
yatteṣāṃ just as
tulya is alike
manyat the capacity of understanding
tathobhayoḥ | of the two
jñāne knowledge
-pi even
sati this is
paśyaitān Look at those
pataṅgāñchā birds
vacañcuṣu || general principle

Then just as in humans, the capacity of understanding exists in all animals, and this is a general principle that the understanding of the two is alike. Look at those birds.

- 52 -

कणमोक्षादृतान्मोहात्पीड्यमानानपि क्षुधा ।
मानुषा मनुजव्याघ्र साभिलाषाः सुतान् प्रति ॥

kaṇamokṣā dṛtānmohāt pīḍyamānānapi kṣudhā |
mānuṣā manu javyāghra sābhilāṣāḥ sutān prati ||

kaṇa food, seeds, grains
mokṣādṛtān ignoring, liberated from
mohāt from attachment
pīḍyamānānapi their own pain
kṣudhā | hunger
mānuṣā humans
manuja vyāghra Supreme Among Men
sābhilāṣāḥ desirous
sutān from their children
prati || in return

Though they have knowledge, because of attachment they are ignoring their own hunger and are busy putting food into the mouths of their children. But Supreme Among Men, humans are different because they are desirous of obtaining reciprocal assistance from their children in their need.

How observant he is to show that all animals and birds wish for their children to grow to independence and continue their lives according to their karma, while only humans desire to maintain a life long relationship and mutual dependence. Humans cultivate bonds of attachment to a much greater extent than any other species.

- 53 -

लोभात्प्रत्युपकाराय नन्वेतान् किं न पश्यसि ।
तथापि ममतावर्त्ते मोहगर्ते निपातिताः ॥

lobhāt pratyupakārāya nanvetān kiṃ na paśyasi |
tathāpi mamatāvartte mohagarte nipātitāḥ ||

lobhāt greed
pratyupakārāya reciprocal assistance
nanvetān in their need
kiṃ what
na can't
paśyasi | you see
tathāpi anyway
mamatāvartte whirlpool of attachment
mohagarte into delusion, ignorance
nipātitāḥ || are hurled into the pit, fall
Can't you see that desire in their greed? People are hurled into the whirlpool of attachment and the pit of delusion

- 54 -

महामायाप्रभावेण संसारस्थिति कारिणा ।
तन्नात्र विस्मयः कार्यो योगनिद्रा जगत्पतेः ॥

mahāmāyā prabhāveṇa saṃsāra sthiti kāriṇā |
tannātra vismayaḥ kāryo yoganidrā jagat pateḥ ||

mahāmāyā by the Great Measurement of Consciousness
prabhāveṇa intrinsic nature, attitude
saṃsāra of all objects in the creation and of their relationships
sthiti circumstance
kāriṇā | cause
tannātra for this there is no
vismayaḥ wonder
kāryo need, cause
yoganidrā the sleep of divine union
jagat of the Universe
pateḥ || the Supreme Lord
by the Great Measurement of Consciousness, who is the cause of the circumstance of all objects in the creation and of their relationships. For this there is no need to wonder. The Consciousness of the Universe, the Supreme Lord, is put into the sleep of divine union

- 55 -

महामाया हरेश्चैषा तया संमोह्यते जगत् ।
ज्ञानिनामपि चेतांसि देवी भगवती हि सा ॥

mahāmāyā hareścaiṣā tayā saṃmohyate jagat |
jñāninnāmapi cetāṃsi devī bhagavatī hi sā ||

mahāmāyā by the Great Measurement of Consciousness
hareścaiṣā Consciousness and
tayā by Her
saṃmohyate is deluded
jagat | the world
jñāninnāmapi of all sensible beings
cetāṃsi the perceiving capacity
devī Goddess
bhagavatī Supreme
hi this
sā || She

by the Great Measurement, and therefore the world is deluded by Her. She, this Supreme Goddess, the Great Measurement of Consciousness, attracts the perceiving capacity of all sensible beings

- 56 -

बलादाकृष्य मोहाय महामाया प्रयच्छति ।
तया विसृजते विश्वं जगदेतच्चराचरम् ॥

balādākṛṣya mohāya mahāmāyā prayacchati |
tayā visṛjate viśvaṃjagadetac carācaram ||

balād with such force
ākṛṣya attracts
mohāya into the ignorance of egotistic attachment
mahāmāyā the Great Measurement of Consciousness
prayacchati | thrust them
tayā from Her
visṛjate is born
viśvaṃ the universe

jagad the perceivable world
etac with all that
carācaram || moves and moves not
with such force as to thrust them into the ignorance of egotistic attachment. The universe is born from Her, the perceivable world with all that moves and moves not,

- 57 -

सैषा प्रसन्ना वरदा नृणां भवति मुक्तये ।
सा विद्या परमा मुक्तेर्हेतुभूता सनातनी ॥

saiṣā prasannā varadā nṛṇām bhavati muktaye |
sā vidyā paramā mukter hetu bhūtā sanātanī ||

saiṣā and it is She who
prasannā after satisfaction
varadā blessing
nṛṇām upon humans
bhavati bestows
muktaye | of liberation
sā She
vidyā knowledge
paramā ultimate
mukter liberation
hetu the cause
bhūtā Existence
sanātanī || the Eternal
and it is She who, after satisfaction, bestows upon humans the blessing of liberation. It is She who is the ultimate knowledge, the cause of the liberation of Consciousness, the Eternal Existence;

- 58 -

संसारबन्धहेतुश्च सैव सर्वेश्वरेश्वरी ॥

saṃsāra bandha hetuśca saiva sarveśvareśvarī ||

saṃsāra to objects and their relationships
bandha the bondage
hetuś the cause

ca and
saiva She is
sarva over all
iśvara over all sovereigns
īśvarī ‖ the full and complete Supreme over all sovereigns.
and She is the cause of the bondage of Consciousness to objects and their relationships, the full and complete Supreme over all sovereigns.

Her name here is Mahamaya. Maha means great and maya means limitation or measurement: the great measurement. It doesn't mean measurement in the sense of a ruler. It means measurement in the sense of a boundary. Every form is a limitation. It limits our consciousness. It divides our perception in space and distinguishes the front of the form from the back, and to the right or to the left of the form. If there were no form there would be unlimited, unqualified, unobstructed consciousness perceiving itself infinitely.

In the Highest Meaning of the Goddess there are three measurements of consciousness, three forms of maya or limitations. As the one in harmony with her own self, there is not a second. As soon as we put one dot or bindu on a plane in space, we have a relationship in front, behind, above, and below. In this way She is the great limitation of consciousness. She measures consciousness by virtue of being a form and then she creates division, a distinction, which spearates it from all other forms. Every form is a container of consciousness. That form is maya.

As soon as we get entrapped by that maya, our Supreme Consciousness goes to sleep and we forget to look beyond the forms to see that the form is a container of consciousness. When we stop looking at the consciousness and look at the forms, our divine consciousness goes to sleep. When She is pleased, She takes our attention away from the outside form and lets us look inside, and then She liberates consciousness. She liberates us from the bondage to form, to the measurement, to the expression, to the manifestation. She grants us freedom. She is the full and complete sovereign over all sovereigns.

- 59 -

राजोवाच ॥

rājovāca ||

rāja the King

uvāca || said:

The King said:

- 60 -

भगवन् का हि सा देवी महामायेति यां भवान् ॥

bhagavan kā hi sā devī mahāmāyeti yāṃ bhavān ||

bhagavan Revered One

kā who

hi is that

sā She

devī Goddess

mahāmāya the Great Measurement of Consciousness

iti of whom, thus

yāṃ bhavān || you speak

Revered One, who is that Goddess, the Great Measurement of Consciousness, of whom you speak?

- 61 -

ब्रवीति कथमुत्पन्ना सा कर्मास्याश्च किं द्विज ।

यत्प्रभावा च सा देवी यत्स्वरूपा यदुद्भवा ॥

bravīti kathamutpannā sā karmāsyāśca kiṃ dvija |

yat prabhāvā ca sā devī yat svarūpā yadudbhavā ||

bravīti tell

katham story

utpannā of Her cause

sā She

karmāsyāś of Her actions

ca and

kiṃ What

dvija | oh Wise One, twice born one

yat by which

prabhāvā attitude

ca and
sā She
devī Goddess
yat what is
svarūpā Her intrinsic nature
yad what
udbhavā || of Her birth
Tell, Oh Wise One, of the actions by which She is known. What is the cause of this Goddess, what is Her intrinsic nature, what of Her birth?

- 62 -

तत्सर्वं श्रोतुमिच्छामि त्वत्तो ब्रह्मविदां वर ॥

tatsarvaṃ śrotumicchāmi tvatto brahma vidāṃ vara ||

tat this
sarvaṃ all
śrotum to hear
icchāmi I wish
tvatto from you
brahmavidāṃ among the Knowers of the One Self-Existent Being
vara || oh Most Excellent
All this I wish to hear from you, Oh Most Excellent among the Knowers of the One Self-Existent Being.

- 63 -

ऋषिरुवाच ॥

ṛṣi ruvāca ||

ṛṣir The Ṛṣi
uvāca || said:
The Ṛṣi said:

- 64 -

नित्यैव सा जगन्मूर्तिस्तया सर्वमिदं ततम् ॥

nityaiva sā jaganmūrtis tayā sarvam idaṃ tatam ||

nitya eternal
eva is verily

sā She
jaganmūrtis the gross world are Her visible forms
tayā by Her
sarvam all
idaṃ tatam || the individual phenomena
She is Eternal, and the gross world and all the individual phenomena in it are Her visible forms. In many ways She is manifest. Hear of them from me.

- 65 -

तथापि तत्समुत्पत्तिर्बहुधा श्रूयतां मम ।
देवानां कार्यसिद्ध्यर्थमाविर्भवति सा यदा ॥

tathāpi tat samutpattir bahudhā śrūyatāṃ mama |
devānāṃ kārya siddhyartham āvirbhavati sā yadā ||

tathāpi nevertheless
tat that
samutpattir She is born
bahudhā in many ways
śrūyatāṃ hear of them
mama | from me
devānāṃ divine ones
kārya perform actions
siddhy for the attainment
artham of this cause, objective
āvirbhavati becomes manifest
sā She
yadā || when

- 66 -

उत्पन्नेति तदा लोके सा नित्याप्यभिधीयते ।
योगनिद्रां यदा विष्णुर्जगत्येकार्णवीकृते ॥

utpanneti tadā loke sā nityāpyabhi dhīyate |
yoganidrāṃ yadā viṣṇur jagat yekārṇa vīkṛte ||

utpanneti is born
tadā then

loke in the world
sā She
nityāpyabhi notwithstanding that She is eternal and unborn
dhīyate | meditated upon, contemplated
yoga divine union
nidrāṃ sleep of
yadā when
viṣṇur Universal Consciousness
jagat the gross world
yekārṇa indistinguishable potentiality, completely united
vīkṛte || at the end of the period for manifestation

- 67 -

आस्तीर्य शेषमभजत्कल्पान्ते भगवान् प्रभुः ।
तदा द्वावसुरौ घोरौ विख्यातौ मधुकैटभौ ॥

āstīrya śeṣamabhajat kalpānte bhagavān prabhuḥ |
tadā dvāvasurau ghorau vikhyātau madhu kaiṭabhau ||

āstīrya rested
śeṣamabhajat at the end of infinity
kalpānte contemplated
bhagavān revered, Supreme
prabhuḥ | Divine Lord
tadā then
dvāvasurau two thoughts
ghorau terrible
vikhyātau known
madhu Too Much
kaiṭabhau || Too Little

- 68 -

विष्णुकर्णमलोद्भूतौ हन्तुं ब्रह्माणमुद्यतौ ।
स नाभिकमले विष्णोः स्थितो ब्रह्मा प्रजापतिः ॥

viṣṇukarṇamalod bhūtau
hantuṃ brahmāṇamudyatau |
sa nābhi kamale viṣṇoḥ sthito brahmā prajāpatiḥ ||

viṣṇu Perceiving Capacity
karṇamalod the dirt of the ears
bhūtau arose
hantuṃ ready to slay
brahmāṇamudyatau | the divine Creative Capacity
sa he
nābhi in the navel
kamale in the lotus blossom
viṣṇoḥ of Consciousness
sthito was seated
brahmā the Creative Capacity
prajāpatiḥ || the Ruler of Beings
65-68. Notwithstanding that She is eternal and unborn, nevertheless when divine ones perform actions for the attainment of this cause, She becomes manifest in the world. At the end of the period for manifestation when the gross world was indistinguishable potentiality, the revered Divine Lord, the Universal Consciousness, rested at the end of infinity in the sleep of divine union. Then from the dirt of the ears of this Perceiving Capacity arose two terrible thoughts, known as Too Much and Too Little. They were ready to slay the divine Creative Capacity, who was seated in the lotus blossom in the navel of Consciousness. The Creative Capacity, the Ruler of Beings,

- 69 -

दृष्ट्वा तावसुरौ चोग्रौ प्रसुप्तं च जनार्दनम् ।
तुष्टाव योगनिद्रां तामेकाग्रहृदयस्थितः ॥

dṛṣṭvā tāvasurau cograu prasuptaṃ ca janārdanam |
tuṣṭāva yoganidrāṃ tāmekāgra hṛdayasthitaḥ ||

dṛṣṭvā seeing
tāvasurau of the two thoughts
cograu the approach
prasuptaṃ asleep
ca and
janārdanam | the Causer of Being

tuṣṭāva indifferently, contentedly
yoganidrāṃ sleep of Divine Union
tāmekāgra with one-pointed attention
hṛdaya heart
sthitaḥ || situated, seated
seeing the approach of the two thoughts and the Causer of Being indifferently asleep in Divine Union, then with one-pointed attention He began to praise Divine Union from His heart.

- 70 -

विबोधनार्थाय हरेर्हरिनेत्रकृतालयाम् ।
विश्वेश्वरीं जगद्धात्रीं स्थितिसंहारकारिणीम् ॥

vibodhanārthāya harer hari netra kṛtālayām |
viśveśvarīṃ jagaddhātrīṃ sthiti saṃhārakāriṇīm ||

vibodhan of awakening
ārthāya For the purpose
harer of Consciousness
hari Consciousness, the Revered One of Brilliant Light, literally who creates, protects, dissolves
netra the eyes
kṛtālayām | extolled
viśveśvarīṃ the Ruler of the Universe
jagaddhātrīṃ Creator of the Perceivable World
sthiti evolution, circumstances
saṃhāra devolution, transformation
kāriṇīm || Cause of
For the purpose of awakening the eyes of Consciousness, the Revered One of Brilliant Light extolled the Ruler of the Universe, Creator of the Perceivable World, Cause of evolution and devolution,

- 71 -

निद्रां भगवतीं विष्णोरतुलां तेजसः प्रभुः ॥

nidrāṃ bhagavatīṃ viṣṇoratulāṃ tejasaḥ prabhuḥ ||

nidrāṃ Sleep
bhagavatīṃ Goddess of
viṣṇor of Consciousness
atulāṃ the unequaled
tejasaḥ Energy, light
prabhuḥ || of the Lord
Goddess of Sleep, the unequaled Energy of Consciousness.

Whenever wise ones get together and perform a sankalpa designed to make Her presence manifest, She becomes manifest in a perceivable form in this world. We can have a relationship with Her. That is what all of us wise ones are doing right now, invoking the Divine Mother in a physical image so we can have a relationship with Her and remember Her. She will give us energy and take away the delusion that comes from being trapped in the whirlpool of maya.

Here all the energy is fully potential energy. There is no kinetic energy. The batteries are fully charged. There is no energy manifested, we perceive total infinite consciousness. Here the Supreme Lord of Universal Consciousness is resting at the end of the ocean of infinity. He is in divine union because there is no second form to perceive.

Here is Vishnu lying on the couch of infinity, Ananta. The snake is the serpent of infinite energy. From Vishnu's navel came a lotus. In the lotus was the Creative Capacity, Brahma. Brahma is sitting there doing his japa in the lotus, in the navel of Supreme Consciousness. From the dirt of the ears come two demons. You know how many dirty things come into our ears and give birth to Too Much and Too Little. We hear things and we start thinking. I don't have enough or I wish that I had more. I have too much and I wish I could get rid of some more.

Dharma and Adharma, action and reaction, positive and negative. Fullness and emptiness. These are some of the dualities. The fact that they are imperceptible doesn't make them devoid of existence. They are existing in the potentiality. All the opposites are present in the potential energy. As soon as one of them manifests, they all spill out and we have too much of something and too little of another thing. That is what allows the creation to manifest. When it is in perfect equilibrium, kamakala, all the threes like AUM, sattva rajas tamas, etc. are in perfect balance. It is called Nirguna because there is no demonstrative quality. Sattva, rajas and tamas are in perfect equilibrium because none is superior to another. That is called nirguna, and when one quality is superior it is called saguna. This means with one particular quality, more than the others. That is how it manifests. That is Her nature.

Sadaa Shiva is pure consciousness, the only existence. That is what happens with Vishnu as he sleeps on the edge of infinity. Shakti is the Divine Mother in full potential energy. Ishwara is the union between Shiva and Shakti or the consciousness and the energy. This is the third principle. Shudda Vidya is Shiva just barely opening his eyes. Shudda Vidya expresses the idea that there may be something out there other than... There may be another existence. The fifth principle is Maya. There is another existence. Too Much and Too Little have been born. After the Maya comes the five kanchukas. Kal, nyati, raga, vidya and kalaa: time, space, attribute, activity, and knowledge. These are modes of perception. That qualified perception gives birth to Purusha, the individual consciousness.

Vishnu is sitting there in divine union and out come Too Much and Too Little who no longer can maintain the equilibrium of perfect balance. Either go and get some more, or go get rid of something you have too much of. Brahma says, "I don't want to fight with you. Fight with someone who is your own size, who is young and strong." They said, "Either you fight with us or vacate that lotus." Brahma said, "Vishnu wake up!" Vishnu was asleep. He wasn't going to wake up for anyone.

Then Brahma began to praise the Divine Mother, Infinite Energy. He said, "Infinite Energy wake up Vishnu from his sleep. Alert consciousness to the impending attack of Too Much and Too Little. They are going to break the equilibrium!"

Remember, it is the Creative Capacity within each of us that is calling out to the Divine Mother. The Creative Consciousness within each of us is calling out to the Supreme Energy, "Please, awaken Supreme Consciousness. I am tired of fighting with Too Much and Too Little. Give me the perfection of balance. Give me the right amount so I can sit still. Let the master of the world rise from his sleep. Let him conquer these two great thoughts for me and beget wisdom."

It is the Creative Consciousness which is desiring this wisdom. Then Brahma sang this hymn. (verses 73-87)

- 72 -

ब्रह्मोवाच ॥

brahmovāca ||

brahma the Creative Capacity
uvāca || said:
The Creative Capacity said:

- 73 -

त्वं स्वाहा त्वं स्वधा त्वं हि वषट्कारः स्वरात्मिका ॥

tvaṃ svāhā tvaṃ svadhā tvaṃ hi
vaṣaṭkāraḥ svarātmikā ||

tvaṃ You
svāhā oblations of I am One with God
tvaṃ you
svadhā oblations of Union with Ancestors
tvaṃ hi You
vaṣaṭkāraḥ oblations of Purity
svar sound
ātmikā || the Consciousness of
You are oblations of I am One with God, you are oblations of Union with Ancestors. You are oblations of Purity, and the Consciousness of all sound.

- 74 -

सुधा त्वमक्षरे नित्ये त्रिधा मात्रात्मिका स्थिता ।
अर्धमात्रास्थिता नित्या यानुच्चार्या विशेषतः ॥

sudhā tvamakṣare nitye tridhā mātrātmikā sthitā |
ardhamātrā sthitā nityā yānuccāryā viśeṣataḥ ||

sudhā Purity
tvam you
akṣare all the letters
nitye eternal
tridhā three
mātrātmikā vowels (A, U, M; aiṃ, hrīṃ, klīṃ), hasya, dirga, pluta
sthitā | circumstance, situated

ardhamātrā half-vowel
sthitā circumstance, situated
nityā eternal
yān its
uccāryā mode of pronunciation
viśeṣataḥ || special

You are the eternal essence of all the letters, and the consciousness of the three vowels (A, U, M; aiṃ, hrīṃ, klīṃ). You are the eternal half-vowel and its special mode of pronunciation.

- 75 -

त्वमेव सन्ध्या सावित्री त्वं देवि जननी परा ।
त्वयैतद्धार्यते विश्वं त्वयैतत्सृज्यते जगत् ॥

tvameva sandhyā sāvitrī tvaṃ devi jananī parā |
tvayai taddhāryate viśvaṃ tvayai tatsṛjyate jagat ||

tvameva you alone
sandhyā the Time of Prayer
sāvitrī the Bearer of the Light
tvaṃ you
devi Goddess
jananī all beings born
parā | above, superior
tvayai by you
tad that
dhāryate sustained, supported
viśvaṃ universe
tvayai by you
tat that
sṛjyate is created
jagat || the perceivable world

You are the Time of Prayer, you are the Bearer of the Light, you are the Goddess above all beings born. The universe is sustained by you, and the perceivable world is created by you.

- 76 -

त्वयैतत्पाल्यते देवि त्वमत्स्यन्ते च सर्वदा ।
विसृष्टौ सृष्टिरूपा त्वं स्थितिरूपा च पालने ॥

tvayaitat pālyate devi tvamatsyante ca sarvadā |
visṛṣṭau sṛṣṭi rūpā tvaṃ sthiti rūpā ca pālane ||

tvayai by you
tat that
pālyate is protected
devi oh Divine Goddess
tvamatsyante you are the end
ca and
sarvadā | always
visṛṣṭau as the Creator
sṛṣṭi of the creation
rūpā form
tvaṃ you
sthitirūpā the form of circumstance
ca and
pālane || its maintenance, protection

You protect what you create, Oh Divine Goddess, and you destroy it in the end. As the Creator, you are the form of the creation, and as the form of circumstance, you are its maintenance.

- 77 -

तथा संहृतिरूपान्ते जगतोऽस्य जगन्मये ।
महाविद्या महामाया महामेधा महास्मृतिः ॥

tathā saṃhṛti rūpānte jagato-sya jaganmaye |
mahāvidyā mahāmāyā mahāmedhā mahāsmṛtiḥ ||

tathā then
saṃhṛtirūpānte at the conclusion as the form of dissolution
jagato-sya of perceivable existence
jaganmaye | you are the All-mighty Measurement of Being, manifestation of perceivable existence

mahāvidyā the Great Knowledge
mahāmāyā the Great Measurement
mahāmedhā the Great Intellect of Love
mahāsmṛtiḥ || the Great Recollection
Then at the conclusion as the form of dissolution of perceivable existence, you are the All-mighty Measurement of Being. The Great Knowledge, The Great Measurement, The Great Intellect, The Great Recollection;

- 78 -

महामोहा च भवती महादेवी महासुरी ।
प्रकृतिस्त्वं च सर्वस्य गुणत्रयविभाविनी ॥

mahāmohā ca bhavatī mahādevī mahāsurī |
prakṛtistvaṃ ca sarvasya guṇa traya vibhāvinī ||

mahāmohā the Great Ignorance
ca and
bhavatī your Ladyship
mahādevī the Great Goddess
mahāsurī | Great Source of Strength
prakṛtis Nature
tvaṃ You
ca and
sarvasya in all
guṇa qualities
traya three
vibhāvinī || manifest
The Great Ignorance too, and your Ladyship, the Great Goddess and Great Source of Strength. You are Nature, and the three qualities that you manifest in all:

- 79 -

कालरात्रिर्महारात्रिर्मोहरात्रिश्च दारुणा ।
त्वं श्रीस्त्वमीश्वरी त्वं ह्रीस्त्वं बुद्धिर्बोधलक्षणा ॥

kāla rātrir mahārātrir moharātriśca dāruṇā |
tvaṃ śrīs tvam īśvarī tvaṃ hrīs
tvaṃ buddhir bodhalakṣaṇā ||

kāla Time
rātrir Night
mahā Great
rātrir Night
moha Ignorance
rātriśca Night
dāruṇā | you are contemplated as
tvaṃ you
śrīs Prosperity, respect
tvam you
īśvarī the Consciousness of All, Seer of All, Supreme Ruler
tvaṃ you
hrīs Humility
tvaṃ you
buddhir Intellect
bodha knowledge
lakṣaṇā || goal, objective
the Night of Time, the Great Night, and the Night of Ignorance. You are Prosperity, you are the Consciousness of All. You are Humility, you are the Intellect, and the goal of all knowledge:

- 80 -

लज्ज्ञा पुष्टिस्तथा तुष्टिस्त्वं शान्तिः क्षान्तिरेव च ।
खड्गिनी शूलिनी घोरा गदिनी चक्रिणी तथा ॥

lajjā puṣṭis tathā tuṣṭis tvaṃ śāntiḥ kṣāntireva ca |
khaḍginī śūlinī ghorā gadinī cakriṇī tathā ||

lajjā modesty
puṣṭis increase, nourishment
tathā then
tuṣṭis satisfaction
tvaṃ you
śāntiḥ Peace
kṣāntir Patient Forgiveness
eva again
ca | and

khaḍginī sword of Wisdom
śūlinī the pike of concentration
ghorā frightful form
gadinī the club of articulation
cakriṇī the discus of revolving time
tathā || then

modesty, increase, then complete satisfaction. You are Peace and Patient Forgiveness. You bear the sword of Wisdom and the pike of concentration, the club of articulation and the discus of revolving time as you present a frightful form.

- 81 -

शङ्खिनी चापिनी बाणभुशुण्डीपरिघायुधा ।
सौम्या सौम्यतराशेषसौम्येभ्यस्त्वतिसुन्दरी ॥

śaṅkhinī cāpinī bāṇabhuśuṇḍī parighāyudhā |
saumyā saumyatarāśeṣa saumyebhyastvati sundarī ||

śaṅkhinī conch of vibrations
cāpinī squasher
bāṇa bow of determination with arrows
bhuśuṇḍī the sling
parighā the iron bar of restraint
yudhā | as a warrior
saumyā mild and gentle
saumyatarāśeṣa the ultimate of attractiveness
saumyebhyas of all who are attractive
tvatisundarī || incomparable beauty

You bear the conch of vibrations and the bow of determination, and other weapons as well. You are mild and gentle and the ultimate of attractiveness and incomparable beauty.

- 82 -

परापराणां परमा त्वमेव परमेश्वरी ।
यच्च किंचित्क्वचिद्वस्तु सदसद्वाखिलात्मिके ॥

parā parāṇāṃ paramā tvameva parameśvarī |
yacca kiṃcit kvacidvastu sadasadvākhilātmike ||

parā above

parāṇāṃ beyond
paramā even again superior
tvameva you alone
parameśvarī | the Supreme Consciousness
yacca whatsoever
kiṃcit various
kvacid and particular
vastu things in existence
sadasadva whether true or untrue
ākhilātmike || in thought or perception

Above and beyond that, and even again superior, you are the Supreme Consciousness. Whatsoever exists in thought or perception, whether true or untrue,

- 83 -

तस्य सर्वस्य या शक्तिः सा त्वं किं स्तूयसे तदा ।
यया त्वया जगत्स्रष्टा जगत्पात्यत्ति यो जगत् ॥

tasya sarvasya yā śaktiḥ sā tvaṃ kiṃ stūyase tadā |
yayā tvayā jagat sraṣṭā jagat pātyatti yo jagat ||

tasya in all
sarvasya everything
yā that
śaktiḥ energy
sā She
tvaṃ you
kiṃ what
stūyase can be sung in your praise
tadā | then
yayā if
tvayā by Her
jagat the perceivable world
sraṣṭā evolution, creates
jagat the perceivable world
pātyatti circumstance, protects

yo this
jagat || the perceivable world
the energy of everything in all is you. Then what can be sung in your praise? If He who is the evolution, circumstance, and devolution of the perceivable world

- 84 -

सोऽपि निद्रावशं नीतः कस्त्वां स्तोतुमिहेश्वरः ।
विष्णुः शरीरग्रहणमहमीशान एव च ॥

so-pi nidrā vaśaṃ nītaḥ kastvāṃ stotumiheśvaraḥ |
viṣṇuḥ śarīra grahaṇa mahamīśāna eva ca ||

so-pi if He
nidrā sleep
vaśaṃ is subject to
nītaḥ have caused
kas what
tvāṃ your
stotu in praise
miheśvaraḥ | devolution, transformation
viṣṇuḥ Maintaining Capacity
śarīra bodies
grahaṇa cause to wear, to accept
mahamīśāna the Dissolving Capacity
eva even (myself)
ca || and
is subject to the sleep that you have caused, then what can be sung in your praise? You cause the Maintaining Capacity and the Dissolving Capacity and myself as well to wear bodies.

- 85 -

कारितास्ते यतोऽतस्त्वां कः स्तोतुं शक्तिमान् भवेत् ।
सा त्वमित्थं प्रभावैः स्वैरुदारैर्देवि संस्तुता ॥

kāritāste yato-tastvāṃ kaḥ stotuṃ śaktimān bhavet |
sā tvamittham prabhāvaiḥ svair
udārairdevi saṃstutā ||

kāritāste for this cause
yato-tastvāṃ hence for this reason
kaḥ who
stotuṃ to sing your praise
śaktimān sufficient ability
bhavet | has
sā She
tvam you
itthaṃ thus
prabhāvaiḥ heavenly, bounteous attitudes
svair your own
udārair manifestations
devi Divine Goddess
saṃstutā || have been extolled
Hence for this reason and for this cause, who has sufficient ability to sing your praise? Oh Divine Goddess, you and your heavenly and bounteous manifestations have been extolled.

- 86 -

मोहयैतौ दुराधर्षावसुरौ मधुकैटभौ ।
प्रबोधं च जगत्स्वामी नीयतामच्युतो लघु ॥

mohayaitau durādharṣā vasurau madhu kaiṭabhau |
prabodhaṃ ca jagat svāmī nīyatāmacyuto laghu ||

mohayaitau the ignorance of egotism
durādharṣā so difficult to understand, so far from the ideal
vasurau upon those two thoughts
madhu Too Much
kaiṭabhau | Too Little
prabodhaṃ awaken, illuminate with knowledge
ca and
jagat of the World
svāmī the Master
nīyatām rouse Him from sleep
acyuto the Consciousness
laghu || Cause

Cause the ignorance of egotism to fall upon those two thoughts so difficult to understand, Too Much and Too Little. Awaken the Consciousness of the Master of the World and rouse Him from sleep.

- 87 -

बोधश्च क्रियतामस्य हन्तुमेतौ महासुरौ ॥

bodhaśca kriya tāmasya hantu metau mahāsurau ||

bodhaś Wisdom, knowledge
ca and
kriya beget
tāmasya of darkness
hantu conquer, slay
metau for me, or within me
mahāsurau || two great thoughts

Let Him conquer these two great thoughts for me and beget Wisdom.

In the fifth Book of Srimad Devi Bagavatam there are 2,500 verses which are a commentary on the seven hundred verses of the Chandi. The story is told that Too Much and Too Little had performed a great tapasya. Brahma came and asked them what boon they wanted and they said, "We want to be eternal." Brahma said. "That's impossible. No one can be eternal. Choose another boon." They said, "We want to be slain in the place where there is no ocean of existence. The ocean of existence covers the entire existence. So we want to be slain in the place where there is no ocean of existence." Brahma said, "Tatastu, I'll give you that boon."

Once they got the boon, Too Much and Too Little started to conquer all of existence. They filled the ocean of existence with strife, making all living beings desire to get more, or striving to get rid of something. Then after they had conquered all of the existence, they decided they wanted to take over Brahma's seat. Now Brahma had given them the boon. He knew he couldn't defeat them. So he called upon the Divine Mother to awaken the consciousness of the master of the world and arouse him from sleep. Let him conquer these two thoughts for me and beget wisdom. If we can put Too Much and Too Little into balance, this is begetting of wisdom.

- 88 -

ऋषिरुवाच ॥

ṛṣi ruvāca ॥

ṛṣi The Ṛṣi
ruvāca ॥ said:
The Ṛṣi said:

- 89 -

एवं स्तुता तदा देवी तामसी तत्र वेधसा ॥

evaṃ stutā tadā devī tāmasī tatra vedhasā ॥

evaṃ thus
stutā praised
tadā then
devī Goddess
tāmasī of Rest, of darkness
tatra there
vedhasā ॥ by the pious worshipper, by the knowledgable one
Thus praised by the pious worshipper, the Goddess of Rest, in order to awaken

- 90 -

विष्णोः प्रबोधनार्थाय निहन्तुं मधुकैटभौ ।
नेत्रास्यनासिकाबाहुहृदयेभ्यस्तथोरसः ॥

viṣṇoḥ prabodhanārthāya
nihantuṃ madhu kaiṭabhau ।
netrāsya nāsikā bāhu hṛdayebhyas tathorasaḥ ॥

viṣṇoḥ of the Supreme Consciousness
prabodhan the awareness
ārthāya in order to, for the purpose of
nihantuṃ to kill
madhu Too Much
kaiṭabhau । Too Little
netrāsya the eyes
nāsikā nose
bāhu arms

hṛdayebhyas heart
tathorasaḥ || and then mouth
the awareness of the Supreme Consciousness to kill Too Much and Too Little, emerged from Her dwelling in the eyes, mouth, nose, arms, chest, and heart.

Just feel Her coming out into a manifest form, coming out from the being of the master of the world. Feel Her wake up. Feel that consciousness waking up inside of you. She is opening those eyes and coming out of your heart, opening up your chest, coming out from your arms. Feel that Goddess giving Her energy to the Supreme Consciousness.

- 91 -

निर्गम्य दर्शने तस्थौ ब्रह्मणोऽव्यक्तजन्मनः ।
उत्तस्थौ च जगन्नाथस्तया मुक्तो जनार्दनः ॥

nirgamya darśane tasthau
brahmaṇo-vyakta janmanaḥ |
uttasthau ca jagannāthas tayā mukto janārdanaḥ ||

nirgamya emerged
darśane became visible
tasthau and then
brahmaṇo to the Creative Capacity
-vyakta of the Unmanifest
janmanaḥ | who is born
uttasthau rose
ca and
jagan of the World
nāthas the Lord
tayā by Her
mukto Freed
janārdanaḥ || the Causer of Being
That immovable, Imperceptible Existence became visible to the Creative Capacity who is born of the Unmanifest. Freed by Her, the Lord of the World, the Causer of Being,

- 92 -

एकार्णवेऽहिशयनात्ततः स ददृशे च तौ ।
मधुकैटभौ दुरात्मानावतिवीर्यपराक्रमौ ॥

ekārṇave-hiśayanāt tataḥ sa dadṛśe ca tau |
madhu kaiṭabhau durātmānā vativīryaparākramau ||

ek Being, oneness
ārṇave on the Ocean of
-hiśayanāt from His couch
tataḥ then
sa He
dadṛśe saw
ca and
tau | those two
madhu Too Much
kaiṭabhau Too Little
durātmānā wicked
vativīrya warriors of great strength
parākramau || marching forward to attack

rose from His couch on the Infinite Ocean of Being. He saw those two wicked warriors of great strength, Too Much and Too Little, marching forward to attack.

- 93 -

क्रोधरक्तेक्षणावत्तुं ब्रह्माणं जनितोद्यमौ ।
समुत्थाय ततस्ताभ्यां युयुधे भगवान् हरिः ॥

krodharaktekṣaṇāvattuṃ brahmāṇaṃ janitodyamau |
samuthāya tatastābhyāṃ yuyudhe bhagavān hariḥ ||

krodha with anger
rakt Red eyed
ekṣaṇ in an instant
āvattuṃ ready to strike
brahmāṇaṃ the Creative Capacity
janitodyamau | they continued in their endeavor to devour, were trying to eat

samuthāya rose
tatas then
tābhyāṃ with the two, with them
yuyudhe and waged battle
bhagavān the Lord
hariḥ || who Removes Confusion

Red eyed with anger and ready in an instant to strike, they continued in their endeavor to devour the Creative Capacity. Then the Lord who Removes Confusion rose and waged battle with the two.

- 94 -

पञ्चवर्षसहस्राणि बाहुप्रहरणो विभुः ।
तावप्यति बलोन्मत्तौ महामायाविमोहितौ ॥

pañca varṣa sahasrāṇi bāhu praharaṇo vibhuḥ |
tāvap yati balon mattau mahāmāyā vimohitau ||

pañca five
varṣa years
sahasrāṇi thousand
bāhu arm in arm, by the arms
praharaṇo wrestled
vibhuḥ | they became
tāvapyati then their own
balon strength
mattau frenzied, crazy
mahāmāyā the Great Measurement of Consciousness
vimohitau || under the delusion, ignorance

For five thousand years the All-Pervading, Omnipresent, Eternal wrestled with them arm in arm, and they became frenzied by their own strength under the delusion of the Great Measurement of Consciousness.

- 95 -

उक्तवन्तौ वरोऽस्मत्तो व्रियतामिति केशवम् ॥

uktavantau varo-smatto vriyatāmiti keśavam ||

uktavantau they told
varo a wish

-smatto of them, from them
vriyatām to choose
iti thus
keśavam || the One of Beautiful Hair
Then they told the One of Beautiful Hair to choose of them a wish.

- 96 -

श्रीभगवानुवाच ॥

śrī bhagavān uvāca ||

śrī bhagavān the Lord of the Universe
uvāca || said:
The Lord of the Universe said:

- 97 -

भवेतामद्य मे तुष्टौ मम वध्यावुभावपि ॥

bhavetāmadya me tuṣṭau mama vadhyā vubhāvapi ||

bhavetāmadya If you are
me with me
tuṣṭau satisfied
mama me
vadhyā tell
vubhāvapi || of your death, how you will die
If you are so satisfied with me, then tell how you will be slain by me.

- 98 -

किमन्येन वरेणात्र एतावद्धि वृतं मम ॥

kimanyena vareṇātra etāvaddhi vṛtaṃ mama ||

kim what
anyena other
vare wish, boon
ṇātra not other
etā this
vaddhi I ask
vṛtaṃ action
mama || me
What other wish could be regarded? This much I ask.

- 99 -

ऋषिरुवाच ॥

ṛṣi ruvāca ||

ṛṣi The Ṛṣi
ruvāca || said:
The Ṛṣi said:

- 100 -

वञ्चिताभ्यामिति तदा सर्वमापोमयं जगत् ॥

vañcitābhyāmiti tadā sarvam āpo mayaṃ jagat ||

vañcitābhyāmiti thus deceived
tadā then
sarvam entire
āpo with the waters
mayaṃ of strife, selfish enjoyment
jagat || the gross world
Thus deceived, they saw that the entire gross world was covered with the waters of strife.

- 101 -

विलोक्य ताभ्यां गदितो भगवान् कमलेक्षणः ।
आवां जहि न यत्रोर्वी सलिलेन परिप्लुता ॥

vilokya tābhyāṃ gadito bhagavān kamalekṣaṇaḥ |
āvāṃ jahi na yatrorvī salilena pariplutā ||

vilokya in the place
tābhyāṃ to him
gadito they said
bhagavān to the Lord
kamalekṣaṇaḥ | with lotus eyes
āvāṃ us
jahi conquer
na yatrorvī is not
salilena by the flood of desire
pariplutā || inundated
Seeing that, they said to the Lord with lotus eyes, "Conquer us in the place that is not inundated by the flood of desire."

Remember Brahma's prayer was to cause the ignorance of egotism to fall upon Too Much and Too Little so that they become intoxicated with their own self importance. And they did. They fought with Vishnu for five thousand years. Vishnu said, "I am very pleased with you both. Choose a boon."

Too Much and Too Little said, "Wait a minute, Vishnu. It is always the stronger that grants boons. We will grant the boon to you. We are not weaker than you. You ask a boon from us."

Vishnu said, "Okay. Tell me how I can slay you both right now. If you don't grant me the boon, then you give up your truth. If you are untrue, you will lose your power."

The whole universe was covered by the flood of desire. Anywhere anyone looked desire would come. Every object they would perceive gave birth to a new desire. Too Little said, "Slay us in a place where there is no desire. Where is there a place that is free from desire?" Vishnu said, "Right here on the lap of consciousness. Sit here where there is no other desire."

- 102 -

ऋषिरुवाच ॥

ṛṣi ruvāca ||

ṛṣi the Ṛṣi
ruvāca || said:
The Ṛṣi said:

- 103 -

तथेत्युक्त्वा भगवता शङ्खचक्रगदाभृता ।
कृत्वा चक्रेण वै च्छिन्ने जघने शिरसी तयोः ॥

tathet yuktvā bhagavatā śaṅkha cakra gadā bhṛtā |
kṛtvā cakreṇa vaicchinne jaghane śirasī tayoḥ ||

tathet let it be so
yuktvā saying
bhagavatā the Glorious One, Supreme Lord
śaṅkha the conch of vibrations
cakra the discus of revolving time
gadā and the club of articulation
bhṛtā | who bears
kṛtvā raised, he performed, did

cakreṇa with the discus of revolving time
vaicchinne severed
jaghane upon His loins
śirasī heads
tayoḥ || the two
Saying, "Let it be so," the Glorious One who bears the conch of vibrations, the discus of revolving time, and the club of articulation, raised the two upon His loins and with the revolutions of time severed their heads.

So they were fooled by Visnu and they sat down on his lap. With his discus of revolving time he cut off their heads.

- 104 -

एवमेषा समुत्पन्ना ब्रह्मणा संस्तुता स्वयम् ।
प्रभावमस्या देव्यास्तु भूयः शृणु वदामि ते ॥

evameṣā samutpannā brahmaṇā saṃstutā svayam |
prabhāvamasyā devyāstu bhūyaḥ śṛṇu vadāmi te ||

evameṣā thus
samutpannā manifested
brahmaṇā by the Creative Capacity
saṃstutā praised
svayam | She Herself
prabhāvamasyā of the Glory, the supreme attitude
devyāstu of the Goddess
bhūyaḥ manifested
śṛṇu listen
vadāmi I speak
te || to you
Thus praised by the Creative Capacity, She manifested Herself. Now I declare more of the Glory of the Goddess. Listen as I speak to you.

This is one example of how She manifested Herself in a perceivable form because of the devotion of the devotee. And now throughout the Chandi, the great Rishi, the Intellect of Love, is going to give us other examples of how She manifests in a perceivable form again and again. Whenever we remember Her and we call on Her with sincere devotion, She will come and take away the energy from adversity and fill us full of Her light, full of Her love, full of Her inspiration, and remove our every difficulty.

ऐं ॐ

aiṃ oṃ

The Pronunciation of Sanskrit Transliteration

a	org*a*n, s*u*m
ā	f*a*ther
ai	*ai* sle
au	s*au*erkr*au*t
b	*b*ut
bh	a*bh*or
c	*c*hur*ch*
ḍ	*d*ough
d	*d*ough slightly toward the *th* sound of *th*ough
ḍh	a*dh* ere
dh	a*dh*ere slightly toward the *theh* sound of brea*the-h*ere
e	pr*ey*
g	*g*o
gh	do*gh*ouse
ḥ	slight aspiration of preceding vowel
h	*h*ot
i	*i*t
ī	pol*i*ce
j	*j*ump
jh	lo*dgeh*ouse
k	*k*id
kh	wor*kh*orse
l	*l*ug
ṃ	resonant nasalization of preceding vowel
m	*m*ud
ṅ	si*ng*
ṇ	u*n*der
ñ	pi*ñ*ata
n	*n*o
o	n*o*
p	*p*ub
ph	u*ph*ill
ṛ	no English equivalent; a simple vowel *r*, such as appears in many Slavic languages
r	*r*oom

ś *sh*awl pronounced with a slight whistle; German *s*prechen
ṣ *sh*un
s *s*un
ṭ *t* omato
t wa*t*er
ṭh *Th*ailand
u p*u*sh
ū r*u*de
v *v*odka midway between *w* and *v*
y *y*es

More Books by Shree Maa and Swami Satyananda Saraswati

Annapūrṇa Thousand Names
Before Becoming This
Bhagavad Gītā
Chaṇḍi Pāṭh
Chaṇḍi Pāṭh Study of Chapter One
Cosmic Pūjā
Cosmic Pūjā Bengali
Devī Gītā
Devī Mandir Songbook
Durgā Pūjā Beginner
Ganeśa Pūjā
Gāyatrī Sahasra Nāma
Gems From the Chaṇḍi
Guru Gītā
Hanumān Pūjā
Kālī Dhyānam
Kālī Pūjā
Lakṣmī Sahasra Nāma
Lalitā Triśati
Rudrāṣṭādhyāyī
Sahib Sadhu
Saraswati Pūjā for Children
Shree Maa's Favorite Recipes
Shree Maa - The Guru & the Goddess
Shree Maa, The Life of a Saint
Śiva Pūjā Beginner
Śiva Pūjā and Advanced Fire Ceremony
Sundara Kāṇḍa
Swāmī Purāṇa
Thousand Names of Ganeśa
Thousand Names of Gayatri
Thousand Names of Viṣṇu and
Satya Nārāyaṇa Vrata Kathā

CDs and Cassettes

Chaṇḍi Pāṭh
Durgā Pūjā Beginner
Lalitā Triśati
Mantras of the Nine Planets
Navarṇa Mantra
Oh Dark Night Mother
Oṃ Mantra
Sādhu Stories from the Himalayas
Shree Maa at the Devi Mandir
Shree Maa in the Temple of the Heart
Shiva is in My Heart
Shree Maa on Tour, 1998
Śiva Pūjā Beginner
Śiva Pūjā and Advanced Fire Ceremony
The Goddess is Everywhere
The Songs of Ramprasad
The Thousand Names of Kālī
Tryambakaṃ Mantra

Videos

Across the States with Shree Maa & Swamiji
Meaning and Method of Worship
Shree Maa: Meeting a Modern Saint
Visiting India with Shree Maa and Swamiji